DISCARD

# Breathe
## Keeping Your Lungs Healthy

Judy Monroe Peterson

New York

Published in 2013 by The Rosen Publishing Group, Inc.
29 East 21st Street, New York, NY 10010

Copyright © 2013 by The Rosen Publishing Group, Inc.

First Edition

All rights reserved. No part of this book may be reproduced in any form without permission in writing from the publisher, except by a reviewer.

### Library of Congress Cataloging-in-Publication Data

Peterson, Judy Monroe.
Breathe: keeping your lungs healthy / Judy Monroe Peterson.—1st ed.
   p. cm.—(Healthy habits)
Includes bibliographical references and index.
ISBN 978-1-4488-6951-0 (library binding)
1. Respiration—Juvenile literature. 2. Lungs—Juvenile literature.—I. Title.
QP121.P48 2013
612.2—dc23

2011048600

*Manufactured in the United States of America*

CPSIA Compliance Information: Batch #S12YA: For further information, contact Rosen Publishing, New York, New York, at 1-800-237-9932.

# CONTENTS

|  | Introduction | 4 |
|---|---|---|
| **CHAPTER 1** | Healthy Lung Basics | 6 |
| **CHAPTER 2** | Avoiding Tobacco and Other Inhaled Drugs | 14 |
| **CHAPTER 3** | Staying Clear of Outdoor Air Pollutants | 26 |
| **CHAPTER 4** | Reducing Air Pollutants at Home | 35 |
| **CHAPTER 5** | A Lifestyle for Healthy Lungs | 43 |
|  | Glossary | 50 |
|  | For More Information | 52 |
|  | For Further Reading | 57 |
|  | Bibliography | 58 |
|  | Index | 61 |

# Introduction

The lungs allow people to laugh, shout, sing, dance, and run. Teens do not usually think about these important organs and what they do. Thanks to the brain, people breathe automatically. The lungs work with other organs to make breathing natural. Sometimes, teens may think about their breathing during strenuous physical activity—for example, when they are swimming or skating fast. People might find breathing more difficult when they are sick. For example, a cough or stuffy nose caused by a cold or the flu might make them breathe poorly.

Most of the time, though, people breathe without thinking about it. The lungs carry out their job all day and all night. From the moment of birth, the lungs work hard. Even when sleeping and dreaming, these organs are essential for keeping a person alive. Healthy or sick, tired or full of energy, you take one breath after another.

The lungs are part of the respiratory system, which is the breathing machine for the body. The role of the lungs is to take in oxygen from the air for the body to use and remove carbon dioxide, a waste product. The body must get oxygen into every cell constantly. Oxygen is critical for turning food into energy for the body.

Breathing is not always the same, however. Different activities affect the breathing rate. When people laugh, they exhale air in a series of quick, short breaths. At the start of a race, the runners' breathing rates speed up in a matter of seconds. They breathe quickly and deeply so that more air travels in and out of the body as they run. After crossing the finish line, the racers slow down and eventually stand still. Their breathing rates return to normal because the lungs do not need to process as much oxygen and carbon dioxide.

# Introduction

Healthy lungs help people maintain a happy and productive life. Breathing is so important that you don't have to think about the process. The body does that automatically.

Taking good care of the lungs will help teens maintain good health throughout life. Healthy lungs come in handy when they, with one big puff, can blow out all of the birthday candles every year.

# Chapter 1

# Healthy Lung Basics

Breathing—also known as respiration—is essential for human life. The respiratory system works with the circulatory system to supply all body cells with oxygen and remove waste. The two lungs of the respiratory system bring in oxygen. The heart and blood vessels of the circulatory system bring oxygen-rich blood to all parts of the body.

According to the American Lung Association (ALA), the average adult breathes in and out about fifteen to twenty times per minute, or more than twenty thousand times each day. Over a lifetime, a person will take about six hundred million breaths. According to *National Geographic*, the lungs bring in 2,100 to 2,400 gallons (8,000 to 9,000 liters) of air each day—enough air to fill a large room. The lungs automatically do this amazing job, along with other important activities.

## The Breathing Body

The lungs are somewhat cone-shaped and fill most of the space in the chest. They act like elastic bags that fill up with and release air. The amount of air the lungs can hold is called lung capacity. A person's lung capacity depends on his or her size, age, gender, and

Healthy Lung Basics

# Diagram of the Human Lungs

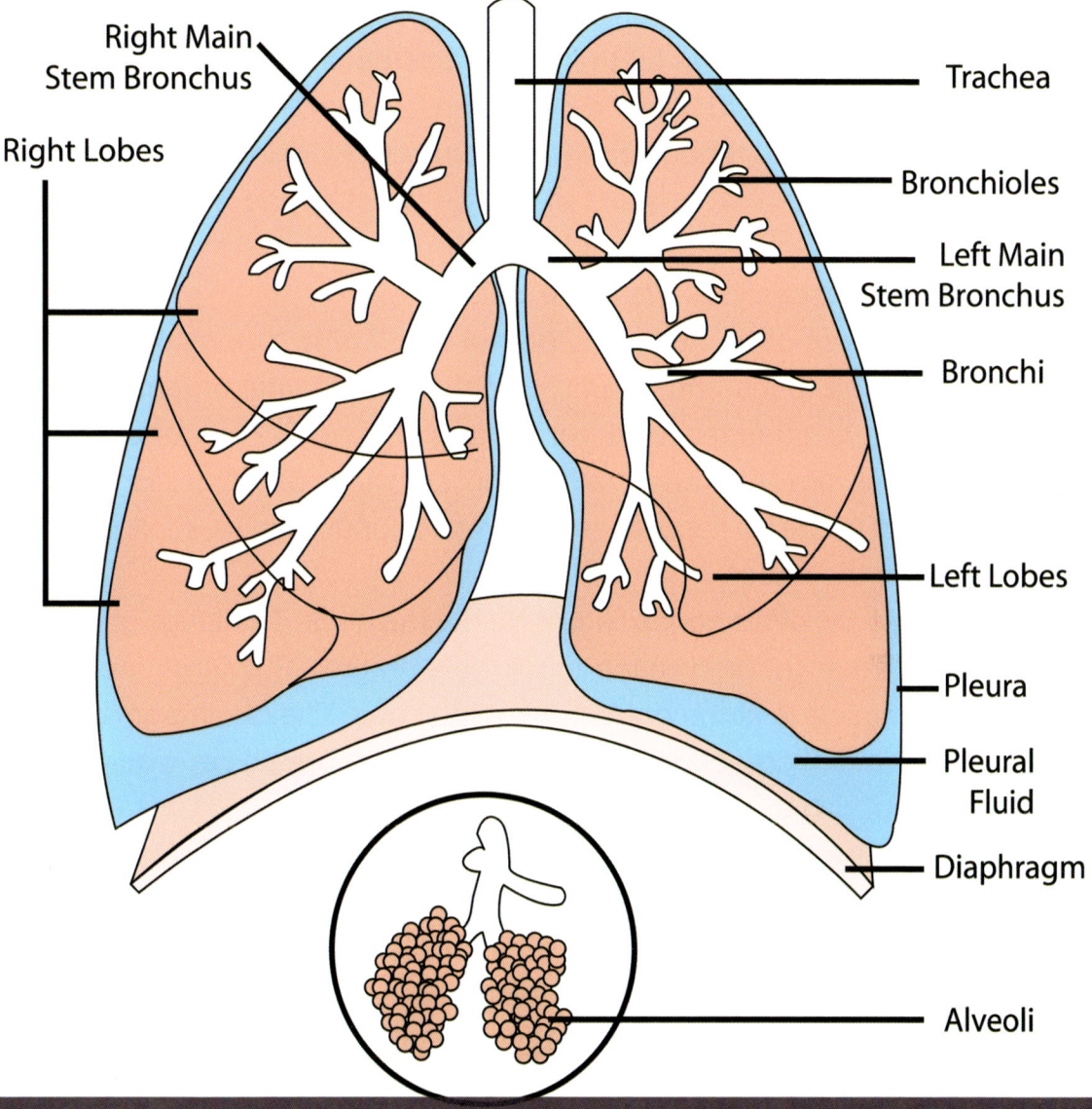

The network of bronchi, bronchioles, and alveoli is known as the bronchial tree. Every time a person breathes in, air travels through the tree, filling many of the millions of alveoli.

other factors. Lung capacity increases until about age twenty-five. Then, as a person ages, lung capacity naturally decreases. The lungs of a typical, healthy adult can hold about 1.1 to 1.6 gal (4 to 6 L) of air when filled to their maximum capacity.

Healthy lungs look squishy like a sponge and are pink on the outside. A thin lining known as the pleural sac covers the outer surface of each of the lungs. The inside of the chest is also lined with a pleural sac. The linings are tough, smooth, and moist. Fluid inside the linings allows the lungs to slide easily within the chest during breathing. On the inside, the left lung has two lobes, or divisions, and the right lung has three. All lobes look the same inside.

Twelve pairs of rib bones inside the chest form a bony cage that surrounds the lungs and heart, protecting these vital organs. Each pair of ribs is attached to a vertebra in the spine. The upper ten pairs of ribs are also attached to the sternum, or breastbone, by cartilage. The heart lies between the two lungs and nestles in the left side of the chest.

The first set of rib bones lie just below the neck. The lungs start at the top of the ribs and reach to the diaphragm. This large, curved sheet of muscle is at the bottom of the rib cage. The diaphragm does much of the work of breathing. Without it, breathing would be impossible.

When a person inhales to draw air into the lungs, the diaphragm tightens and straightens. It moves down as muscles supporting the ribs pull up and out. The lungs stretch out like balloons and air rushes into them. During exhalation, the diaphragm relaxes and curves up. As the rib muscles push down and in, the lungs get smaller and force air out of the body. When people breathe normally, the diaphragm moves up and down about half an inch (about 13 millimeters). When exercising, the diaphragm may move up and down as much as 3 to 4 in. (76 to 102 mm).

## The Gas Exchange Process

Working together, the respiratory system and the circulatory system exchange gases between the body and the environment. The lungs fill with air and transfer oxygen to the blood. The heart pumps the oxygen-rich blood to every cell of the body through the arteries. Blood containing carbon dioxide travels through the veins to the heart, where it is pumped to the lungs. The lungs remove carbon dioxide from the blood and replace it with oxygen. The oxygen-rich blood travels to the heart and the cycle continues.

The process begins when air is inhaled. Air enters the body mainly through the nose and sometimes through the mouth. The air flows into the pharynx, or throat. The lower part of the pharynx splits into two tubes. One tube, the esophagus, is for food and drink and leads to the stomach. The second tube is the trachea, or windpipe. Food doesn't enter the windpipe because a flap of cartilage called the epiglottis closes off the entrance to the trachea.

Toward the middle of the chest, the trachea splits into two narrower tubes called the bronchi. Each bronchial tube enters one lung, where it divides into the bronchioles. These small tubes end in hundreds of millions of alveoli. These tiny air sacs look like clusters of grapes. Capillaries (tiny blood vessels) surround the alveoli. It is here that oxygen filters into the blood. Oxygen and carbon dioxide easily move through the thin walls of the alveoli and capillaries.

Oxygen moves from the alveoli into the bloodstream through the capillaries. Some of the capillaries connect to the pulmonary veins.

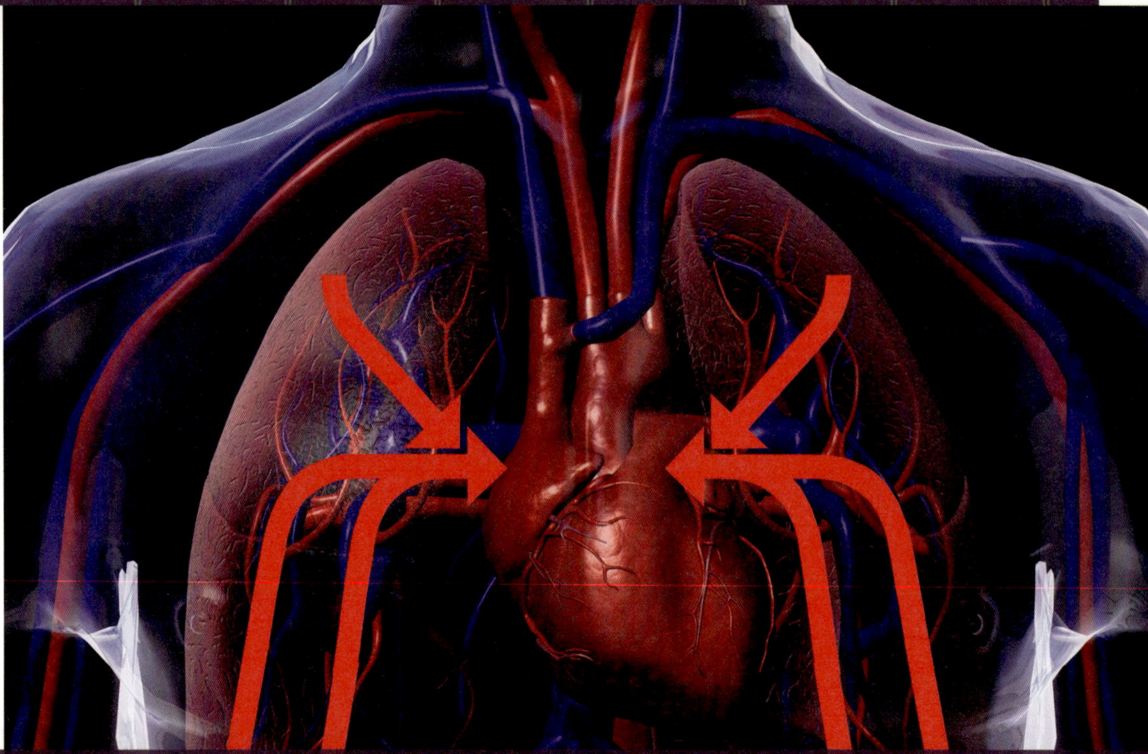

# Breathe: Keeping Your Lungs Healthy

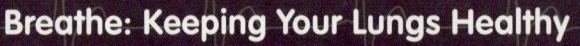

The lungs pass oxygen from the air to the blood. Then the heart quickly pumps the oxygen-rich blood through the body. Blood can travel from the heart to the big toe and back in under one minute.

These special veins carry the oxygen from the lungs to the heart. There, the oxygen-rich blood is pumped out through the arteries to all of the cells and tissues of the body. Oxygen combines with substances in food to release energy for the body to use for all of its activities, such as thinking, reading, exercising, eating, and resting.

As energy is created, carbon dioxide is produced. This waste gas passes out of the cells and tissues into the bloodstream and travels through the veins back to the heart. The heart pumps this oxygen-poor, waste-rich blood back to the lungs through the pulmonary arteries. This blood reaches the capillaries surrounding the alveoli. Here, carbon dioxide from the blood is released and replaced with oxygen. The carbon dioxide passes through the thin walls of the alveoli and travels to the bronchi. It then moves up the trachea and is exhaled through the nose or mouth. The gas exchange cycle continues automatically. This process is critical because too much carbon dioxide in the blood can harm the organs in the body.

## Other Jobs of the Lungs

In addition to breathing, the lungs perform other important tasks. One job is to regulate the temperature of air to body temperature. If needed, the lungs add moisture to inhaled air.

The lungs and other parts of the respiratory system also help keep people from getting sick. The air people breathe is a mixture of gases.

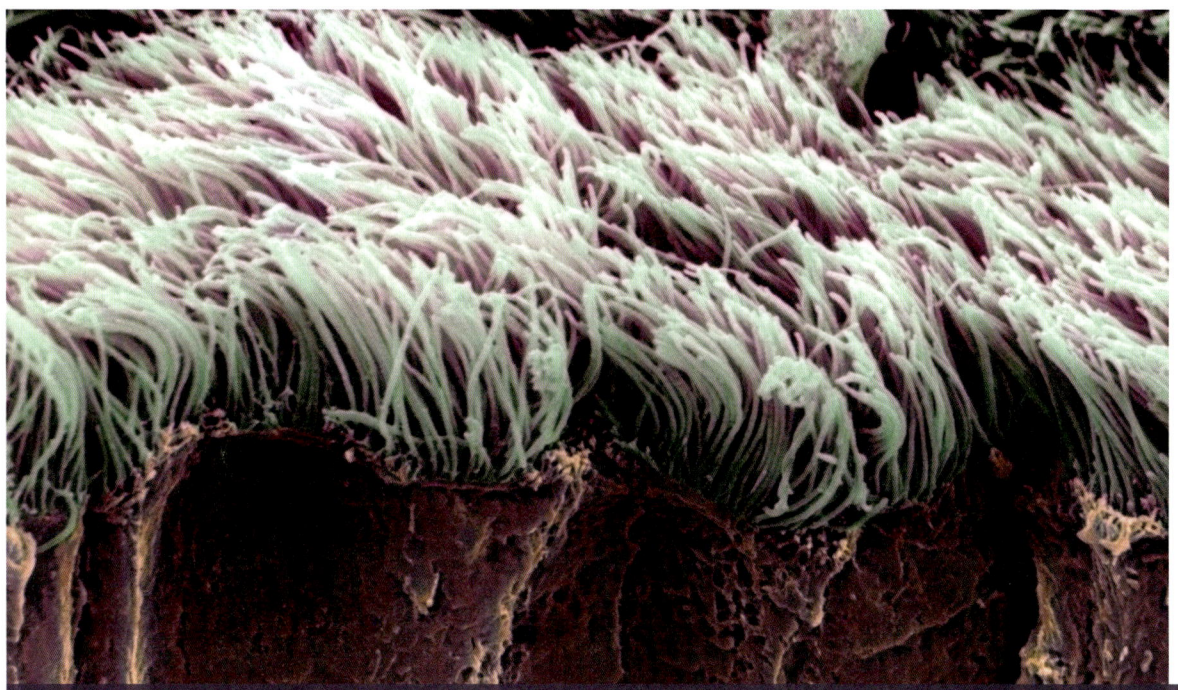

In this photograph, the hairlike cilia are magnified with an electron microscope and colored green and pink. As air is inhaled, the cilia sweep back and forth to keep unwanted substances from entering the lungs.

**Breathe: Keeping Your Lungs Healthy**

It can also include harmful substances such as bacteria, viruses, dust, and pollutants. A sticky fluid called mucus lines the nose and trachea and traps most of the unwanted materials that enter through the nose and mouth. Tiny, hairlike cilia line the bronchial tubes and move together in waves to push mucus mixed with germs and dirt up into the nose. People get rid of the mucus by coughing, blowing their nose, or sneezing.

Sometimes, harmful matter gets through the trachea and enters the lungs. Then special cells called macrophages swing into action. They surround and destroy the harmful material. The lungs also help clean the blood of certain harmful substances.

## Lungs and Speech

People would not be able to speak, sing, or cheer on their favorite teams without the airways and lungs. The larynx, or voice box, is located at the top of the trachea. The vocal cords, which lie near the base of the larynx, form a V-shaped opening called the glottis. During regular breathing, air passes through this gap. Sound is produced when the cords close together and vibrate as air from the lungs passes between them. This action creates the sounds needed for speech or humming.

## A Delicate Balance

The lungs are among the largest organs in the body, but they are delicate. Because they process air, they are constantly exposed to bacteria and viruses from the environment. These microorganisms can cause people to become infected with a cold, the flu, or pneumonia.

Other factors, such as smoking, can contribute to lung and breathing problems. Teens who smoke are at increased risk for developing serious diseases. Over time, tobacco smoke can cause the tubes inside the lungs to become partially blocked. The narrowing of these tubes can lead to obstructive lung diseases, such as emphysema. Smoking can also result in lung cancer. The National Institutes of Health (NIH) lists lung cancer as the leading cause of cancer death in both men and women in the United States.

Air pollution also poses problems for the lungs. It contributes to lung cancer and can make breathing more difficult for people, including those who have asthma.

Teens can look after their lungs in many ways. Staying away from harmful air pollutants helps the lungs work well. Teens can also make lifestyle changes to help their lungs stay healthy. Keeping fit, for example, keeps the lungs strong, allowing people to take in more oxygen in a single breath. Small changes can also help, such as brushing the teeth at least twice a day to remove germs that could move from the mouth to the lungs. Teens can develop and follow healthy habits to help their lungs work well now and in the future.

# Chapter 2
## Avoiding Tobacco and Other Inhaled Drugs

All drugs are powerful chemical substances that can affect the body in many ways. Some drugs help cure, prevent, or treat diseases, injuries, and other medical problems. Other drugs, such as marijuana and cocaine, are harmful to the lungs and other parts of the body. Marijuana and cocaine are illegal to sell and use.

The most commonly inhaled drug is the nicotine found in tobacco. Although tobacco products like cigarettes are legal, in most states only people eighteen and older are permitted to buy them.

Some people use inhalants as drugs. Inhalants are chemicals that have a wide range of household uses, but people sometimes misuse them to get high. This is an extremely dangerous practice.

## Cigarette Smoking and the Lungs

The lungs and other parts of the respiratory system are highly sensitive to tobacco smoke. Smoking can cause serious health problems and even death. According to the Centers for Disease Control and Prevention (CDC), cigarette smoking results in more than 443,000 deaths in the United States every year. The CDC also reports that smoking is the leading cause of avoidable deaths, disability, and disease in the United States.

With each puff, smokers inhale more than forty chemicals known to cause cancer. People quickly become addicted to nicotine, a drug

Smoke inhaled into the lungs decreases the lungs' efficient transfer of oxygen and carbon dioxide. The poisonous gases from smoke go right into the lungs and then into the bloodstream.

found in tobacco. When people inhale cigarette smoke, nicotine is absorbed into the blood. The drug speeds up the respiratory system, the circulatory system, and other body systems. The lungs are forced to work harder.

The flavor of a cigarette comes from the tar in tobacco. Tar is a dark, thick, and sticky substance. It travels into smokers' airways and lungs and damages or destroys the cilia. Mucus builds up, and people continually cough to try to clear their airways. In time, they may develop breathing diseases. Eventually, tar causes the lungs to lose their elasticity, or ability to expand and contract.

Carbon monoxide in cigarette smoke passes through the lungs into the blood. This poisonous gas has no color or odor. Because carbon monoxide moves into the blood, less oxygen is carried to the body's cells.

## Lung Diseases

Over time, smoking can cause or worsen lung diseases, including chronic bronchitis, emphysema, cystic fibrosis, and lung cancer.

In chronic (ongoing) bronchitis, the lining of the bronchi becomes irritated and inflamed, and extra mucus is produced. The lining of the airways becomes thickened, and the cilia become useless. As a result, less air is able to flow to and from the lungs. Bacteria and viruses that reach the bronchi are not removed and can cause infection more easily. People who have chronic bronchitis cough a lot and are short of breath when playing sports, doing exercises, or just walking up stairs.

In emphysema, the alveoli become stretched and permanently filled with air. The lungs become less elastic and lose much of their ability to provide oxygen for the body. People find it more difficult to breathe and cough often. Together, emphysema and chronic bronchitis are known as chronic obstructive lung disease (COPD). According to the ALA, COPD is the fourth leading cause of death in the United States.

Cystic fibrosis is an inherited disease (a disease passed down through families). In this disease, thick, sticky mucus builds up in the lungs and digestive tract. The mucus plugs up the passageways and tubes, especially in the lungs. People with cystic fibrosis have difficulty breathing and digesting food. This life-threatening disorder is one of the most common chronic lung diseases in children and young adults.

Lung cancer is deadly and is directly linked to cigarette smoking. The National Institute on Drug Abuse (NIDA) reports that cigarette

# Avoiding Tobacco and Other Inhaled Drugs

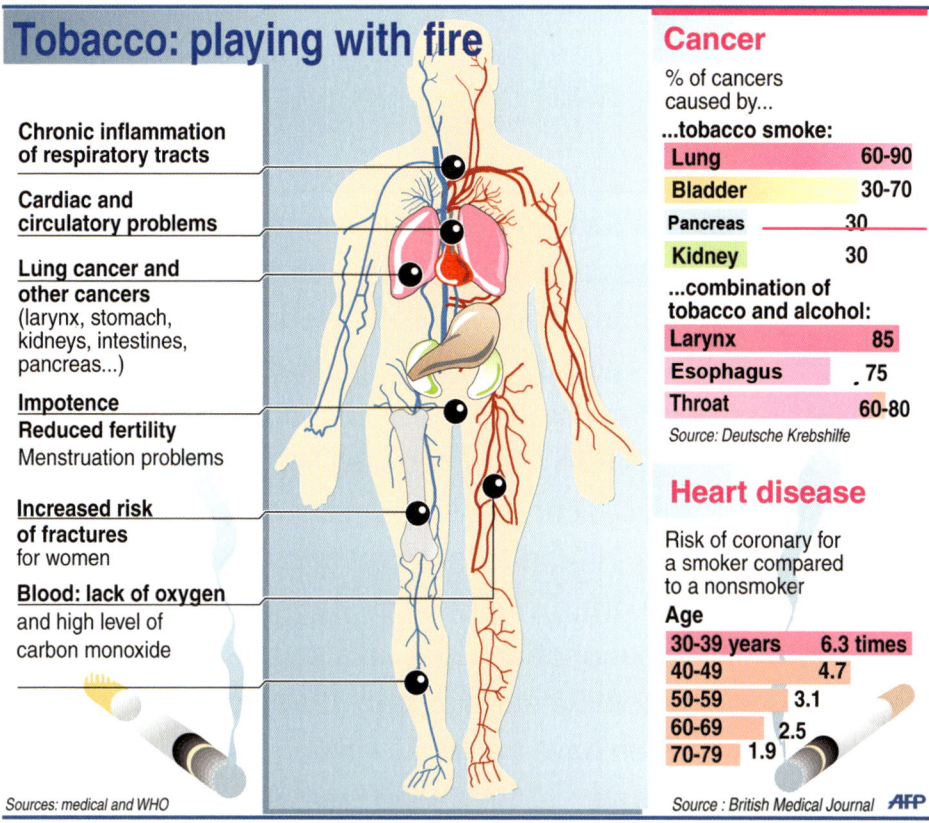

## Tobacco: playing with fire

- **Chronic inflammation of respiratory tracts**
- **Cardiac and circulatory problems**
- **Lung cancer and other cancers** (larynx, stomach, kidneys, intestines, pancreas...)
- **Impotence**
- **Reduced fertility** Menstruation problems
- **Increased risk of fractures** for women
- **Blood: lack of oxygen** and high level of carbon monoxide

Sources: medical and WHO

### Cancer
% of cancers caused by...
...tobacco smoke:

| | |
|---|---|
| Lung | 60-90 |
| Bladder | 30-70 |
| Pancreas | 30 |
| Kidney | 30 |

...combination of tobacco and alcohol:

| | |
|---|---|
| Larynx | 85 |
| Esophagus | 75 |
| Throat | 60-80 |

Source: Deutsche Krebshilfe

### Heart disease
Risk of coronary for a smoker compared to a nonsmoker

| Age | |
|---|---|
| 30-39 years | 6.3 times |
| 40-49 | 4.7 |
| 50-59 | 3.1 |
| 60-69 | 2.5 |
| 70-79 | 1.9 |

Source: British Medical Journal  AFP

---

Tobacco use is a high-risk behavior that can lead to serious health consequences. The health risks begin from the moment the first cigarette is lit and the smoke enters the body.

---

smoking causes about one-third of all cancers and 80 to 90 percent of lung cancer, the number-one cancer killer in the United States. More men and women die from lung cancer than any other form of cancer. Smokers hurt their lungs and heart each time they light up. The longer a person smokes, the worse the damage becomes.

The only sure way to avoid addiction to nicotine is to avoid smoking. Never start this unhealthy habit. If people quit smoking, their physical fitness increases because they can breathe more easily. In addition, their chances of lung and heart disease decrease.

## Secondhand Smoke

Even if teens do not smoke, they might be exposed to secondhand smoke. Nonsmokers can inhale the smoke that travels from the ends of burning cigarettes, cigars, or pipes, as well as the smoke that smokers exhale. A room filled with smoke contains many of the same poisons and cancer-causing substances that are in cigarettes.

Inhaling secondhand smoke increases a person's risk of developing lung cancer. The NIDA estimates that secondhand smoke causes three thousand lung cancer deaths per year among people who have never smoked. Secondhand smoke can cause nonsmokers to cough a lot and produce extra mucus, which causes breathing difficulties. People exposed to secondhand smoke also tend to get more respiratory infections and asthma attacks than other people. For this reason, many cities and states have banned smoking in public places, including schools, hospitals, stores, and restaurants, and on public transportation. A federal law bans smoking on American airplanes.

## Marijuana and Cocaine

Marijuana and cocaine harm the body in many ways. They change the way the brain works so that it does not receive and respond to information correctly. This can affect the entire body, including the respiratory, nervous, and circulatory systems.

Marijuana is usually smoked in a cigarette (known as a joint), a hollowed-out cigar (known as a blunt), or a water pipe (known as a bong). The smoke contains more cancer-causing substances than tobacco smoke. When smoked, marijuana produces more than two thousand chemicals that enter the body through the lungs. Within a few minutes of inhaling the drug, the heartbeat speeds up and blood pressure rises, causing redness in the eyes. The smoke irritates the lungs, and the mouth and throat become dry. Coordination, balance, and memory are soon affected. Ongoing use of marijuana can result in daily coughing, production of excess mucus, wheezing, difficulty breathing, and chest pain. Users tend to get colds and other respiratory illnesses easily. By damaging their lungs, they increase their risk of developing chronic bronchitis and other lung diseases.

Cocaine is highly addictive. People usually take the white powder by snorting (inhaling) it into the nose, where it is then absorbed into the blood. The pure form of cocaine, called crack, is smoked in a pipe. The smoke is inhaled into the lungs. Using cocaine has many effects on the body, such as an increase in heart rate and blood pressure and irregular heartbeat. Users might have shortness of breath, headaches, stomach pain, and nausea. Over time, snorting cocaine can lead to loss of one's sense of smell, hoarseness, a constantly running nose, nosebleeds, and swallowing problems. Smoking crack irritates the lungs, resulting in constant coughing and chronic bronchitis, and it can damage them permanently. In any form, cocaine use can cause sudden death by breathing failure, heart attack, or stroke.

## Inhalants

People come across inhalants regularly: many are cleaning products and other common household products. They are often a mix of poisonous chemicals and have a strong smell. These products are usually safe when used for their intended purpose and with good ventilation. However, some people abuse inhalants by purposely breathing them in to get high.

# Breathe: Keeping Your Lungs Healthy

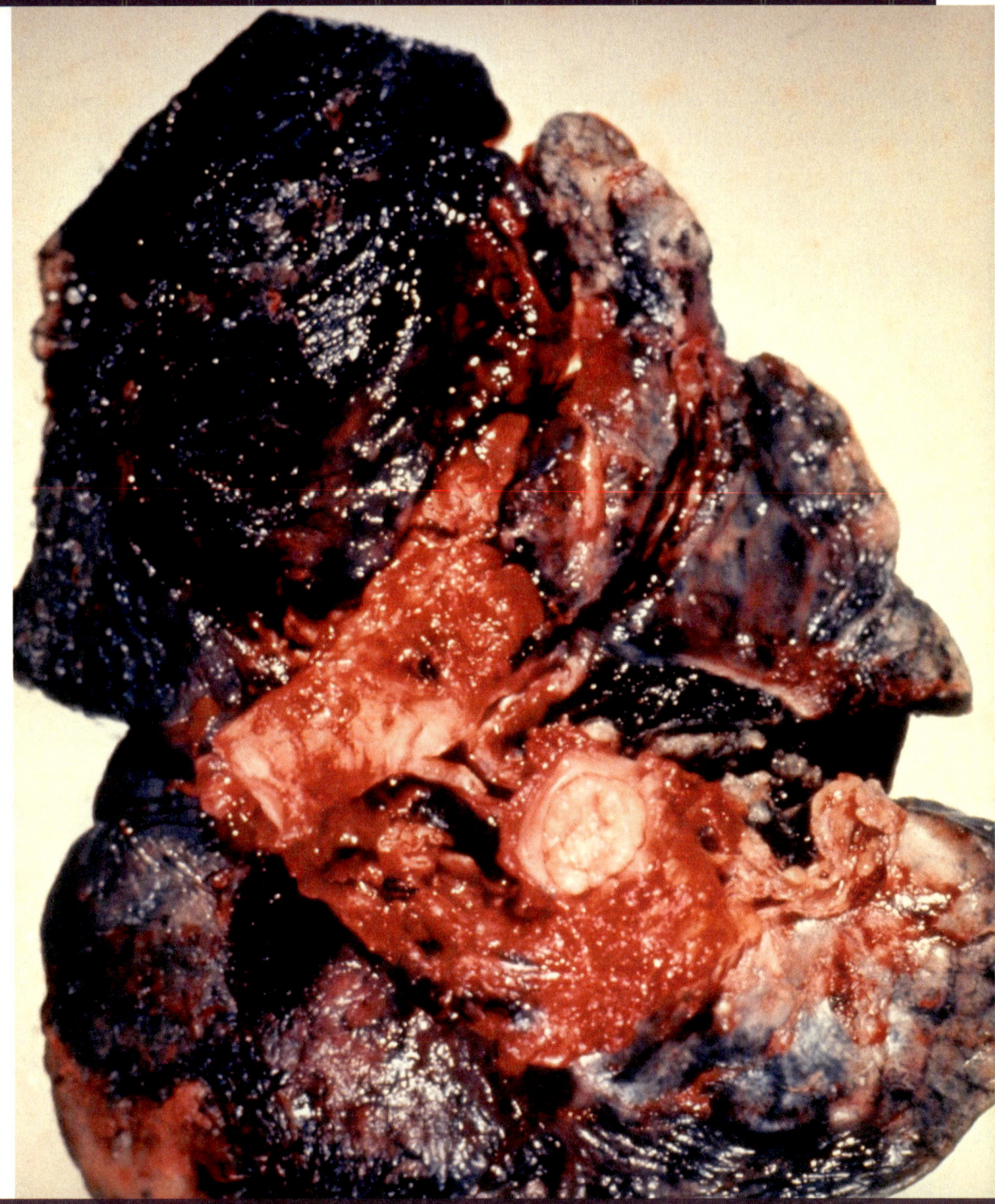

Lung cancer is directly linked to cigarette smoking. As in the sample above, the lung tissue becomes damaged and blackened with thick, dark tar. White areas show where lung cancer has developed.

# Avoiding Tobacco and Other Inhaled Drugs

More than one thousand products have chemicals that can be inhaled through the mouth (known as huffing) or through the nose (known as sniffing). Inhalants fall into several groups, including solvents, aerosols, and gases. Solvents are liquids that can dissolve other substances and are easily vaporized (changed into a gas). Inhalants in this group include gasoline, lighter fluid, paint thinner, glue, and nail polish remover. Aerosols are sprays that contain propellants, or substances that help push out the product. Examples include hair spray, cooking spray, and spray paint. Computer cleaning products are a common, and particularly dangerous, aerosol inhalant. The substance in whipped cream dispensers, refrigerant gases, and medical anesthetics are among the gases that people inhale.

Inhalants impact the whole body. When someone huffs or sniffs, the poisonous fumes rush into the lungs and then into the blood. The blood carries the poisons throughout the body. Some chemicals

## Sudden Sniffing Death

Inhalants are scary because even a healthy person can die from abusing them just once or a few times. This is called sudden sniffing death, and it can happen within minutes. Sometimes, the gases from the inhalant fill the cells in the lungs with poisonous chemicals. Little or no room is left for the oxygen needed to breathe. The respiratory system then fails and death occurs. Because inhalants can cause the heart to beat too fast, users can also die from a sudden heart attack.

leave the body through the lungs, kidneys, and skin. Others are stored in the fatty tissue of the brain, nervous system, liver, kidneys, heart, and muscles. Users might develop a constant cough, feel numb and tired, and get bad headaches and stomach pains. They can seriously damage their lungs and cause permanent breathing problems. Using inhalants can damage the brain permanently. It can also lead to death.

## Choosing to Be Drug-Free

In addition to damaging their lungs, users who smoke, take illegal drugs, or use inhalants may become addicted. Using drugs then becomes the focus of their lives, since they can't function without them. Addiction can happen with many types of substances, including nicotine, marijuana, cocaine, crack, and inhalants.

When people are dependent on and continue to use a drug even though they know it causes harm, they have an addiction. They might develop a psychological addiction—the desire to keep taking a drug to get its effects. Users can also become physically addicted to a drug. A physical addiction causes withdrawal, or uncomfortable symptoms from the body ridding itself of the drug, if the user stops taking it. If teens stop taking a drug, they might feel sick, shaky, irritable, and anxious. Depending on the drug, withdrawal can also produce headaches, sweating, muscle cramps, stomach pains, and nausea. Often, users have both a psychological and a physical addiction to a drug. Some substances are highly addictive, such as crack cocaine. Smoking this drug even once or a few times can lead to addiction.

Drug use has many harmful effects on the brain and the respiratory, circulatory, and other body systems. Drugs are especially dangerous for teens because their bodies are still growing. To stay

Purposely sniffing products such as spray dusters, made for cleaning electronic equipment, is dangerous. Not enough oxygen can get through the lungs into the bloodstream. It can also severely damage the lungs.

# Breathe: Keeping Your Lungs Healthy

healthy, teens can choose not to try or use drugs in the first place. Breaking a drug habit or addiction can be done, but many people find it difficult. For example, cigarette smokers might have to try a number of approaches over time to stop smoking. Smoking cessation (quitting smoking) groups and drug detox programs can help people break their addiction. Other treatments include crisis intervention and hospital, clinical, and private programs. Staying clear of drugs is the best way to avoid the dangers of addiction and help keep the lungs and other organs healthy.

# MYTHS and FACTS

**MYTH:** Both lungs are the same size.

**FACT:** To make room for the heart, the left lung is smaller than the right lung.

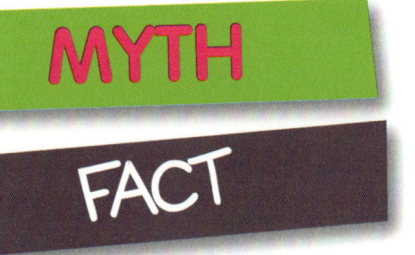

**MYTH:** A person who has a damaged or diseased lung cannot receive a new one.

**FACT:** Lung transplantation (lung replacement) is surgery to replace one or more lobes of a lung, or one or both diseased lungs, with healthy lungs from a donor. The surgeon removes the diseased lung and attaches the new lung to the main blood vessels and air passages. This procedure can extend some people's lives. However, a lung transplant is a complex treatment with high risks, and it cannot be used for all patients with advanced lung disease.

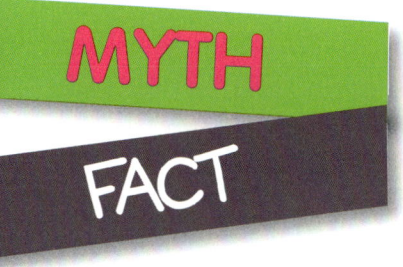

**MYTH** People can completely exhale all of the air in their lungs.

**FACT** After a normal exhalation, a bit more air can be forced out of the lungs. This air is known as reserve air. However, about 2.5 pints (1.2 liters) of air stays in the lungs all the time. This air is known as residual air, and it cannot be forced out by breathing.

# Chapter 3

# Staying Clear of Outdoor Air Pollutants

Air quality affects how people live and breathe. Breathing clean air helps people stay healthy. The outdoor air that some teens breathe, though, contains many kinds of pollutants. Inhaling polluted air can lead to short-term health problems. People might have burning eyes and nose, headaches, coughing, sneezing, a sore throat, and dizziness. Once they breathe clean air, these effects tend to go away.

The effects of exposure to air pollutants over a long period of time often cannot be reversed. People might start to wheeze, cough, and have difficulty breathing. Because the lungs cannot function well, existing respiratory problems can become worse, or lung cancer can develop.

## Common Air Pollutants

Air pollution is the contamination of air by harmful substances—substances that produce discomfort or harm to living things or the environment. Sometimes pollution is visible, such as smog hanging over a city. Smog—a combination of the words "smoke" and "fog"—occurs when sunlight acts on air polluted by smoke and vehicle exhaust fumes. In the presence of strong sunlight, substances in the

Smog often appears as a yellowish brown haze in the air. When smog levels rise, the number of people experiencing breathing problems increases.

polluted air react to form ozone. A major contributor to smog is the burning of coal by power plants to produce electricity.

Human beings produce most of the wastes that cause air pollution. Most of these wastes are in the form of gases or particulates (substances made up of tiny particles). These substances result mainly from burning fossil fuels such as oil, coal, wood, and natural gas. Fossil fuels power motor vehicles, airplanes, and other motor transportation. Factories and the burning of garbage also contribute to air pollution.

## Gases That Pollute

People survive by breathing in a mix of gases, mainly oxygen and nitrogen. Many things that make people's lives more comfortable, such as cars, electricity, and heating, create unwanted gases. These gases include carbon dioxide, carbon monoxide, sulfur dioxide, and nitrogen oxides.

Carbon dioxide is a major air pollutant that results from the burning of fossil fuels. The fumes created by motor vehicles, motorboats, planes, jets, and lawnmowers contain this gas. Power plants and cigarette smoke are other sources. The lungs absorb this poison, preventing the body from receiving enough oxygen. People may then have headaches and feel dizzy. If a person inhales too much carbon dioxide—deep in a coal mine, for example—the respiratory system may stop working and death will occur.

The exhaust fumes of motor vehicles also contain carbon monoxide. Other sources of this gas are power plants, cigarette smoke, and wood-burning stoves or fireplaces. Carbon monoxide has no smell,

Polluting clouds of car exhaust rise into the air at a stoplight. People may not always see exhaust fumes, but all motor vehicles emit them.

color, or odor. When inhaled, the gas enters the bloodstream and replaces some of the oxygen in the blood. The delivery of oxygen to the body's organs, tissues, and cells is decreased. People can develop headaches and feel tired, dizzy, and confused. Extremely high levels of carbon monoxide can block the delivery of oxygen to the cells, causing the respiratory system to stop working. Death can occur quickly and without warning. Today, many people install carbon monoxide detectors in their homes for safety.

The burning of coal, oil, and other fossil fuels produces sulfur dioxide and nitrogen oxides. These gases irritate the respiratory system, causing coughing, burning and tearing eyes, and increased mucus production. Over time, inhaling nitrogen oxides can lead to chronic bronchitis and can increase the risk of serious lung infections such as pneumonia. In addition, nitrogen oxides contribute to the formation of ozone, the main component of smog. When ozone close to the ground reaches high levels, it is dangerous to people's health. The lungs can become irritated and damaged, reducing their ability to work well. In addition, the lungs can become more sensitive to other irritants in the air.

## Particulates

Besides gases, another major source of air pollution is particulate matter. Particulates, made up of extremely small particles and liquid droplets, come from natural sources such as forest fires and wind erosion. Motor vehicles, factory smokestacks, building and road construction, and farming can also cause particulates to form.

The smaller the particle, the more easily it can be inhaled and travel deep into the lungs. These substances can settle on the walls of the trachea, bronchi, and bronchioles and may reach the alveoli. If the body cannot get rid of the particulates, the action of the cilia decreases over time. The lungs become irritated and damaged and cannot work efficiently. People might cough a lot, have difficulty breathing, and are at increased risk of developing serious lung diseases such as chronic bronchitis, emphysema, and some cancers.

Metals like lead are released into the air through motor vehicle exhaust, mining, burning of waste, and manufacturing. Lead can last

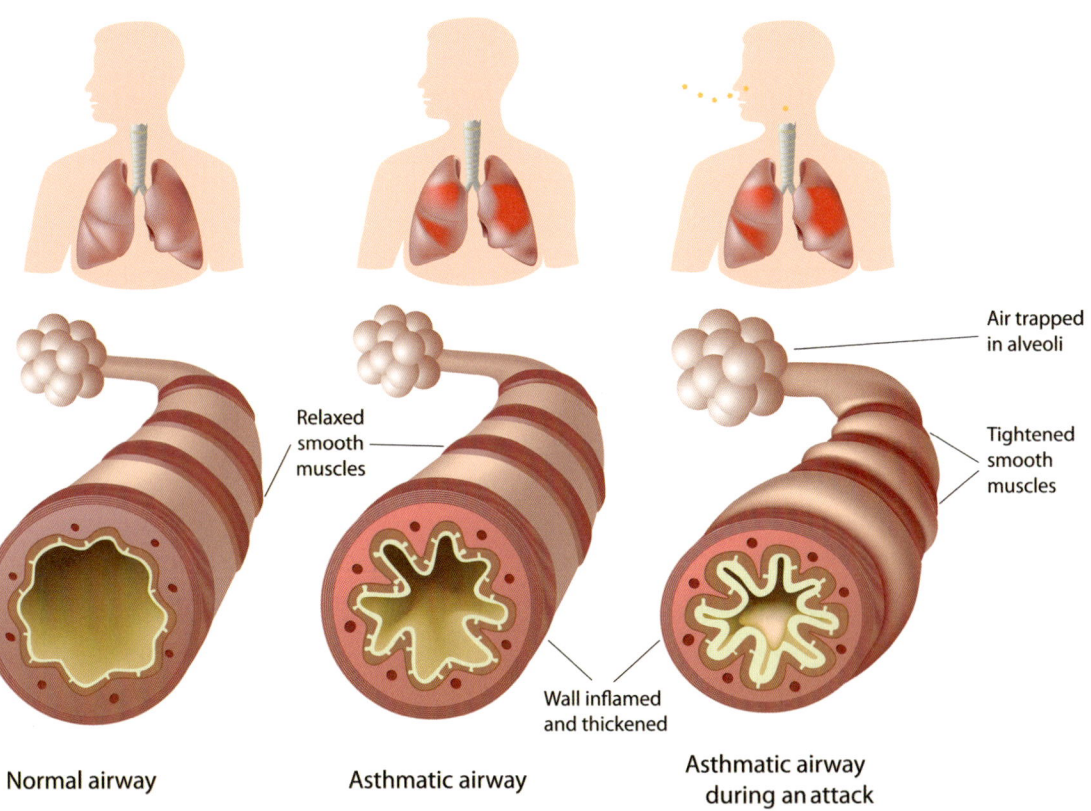

**Changes Produced by Asthma**

During an asthma attack, the airways are irritated and inflamed (swollen). As a result, it is harder to get air into and out of the lungs.

a long time in the body because it collects in the bones and tissues. Damage to the nervous system, kidneys, liver, and bones can occur.

## Effects on Asthma

Asthma is a chronic disease that causes the airways to narrow. People who have asthma frequently have irritated airways. Their airways react to different irritants in the environment by swelling and filling with mucus. The muscles around the airways may also tighten up. These changes make it difficult for air to move into and out of the lungs. People then have coughing, wheezing, chest pain, and shortness of breath. Sudden asthma attacks can cause people to gasp for air and feel as if they cannot breathe. Many people with asthma carry "rescue" medications (often taken through an inhaler) that cause their airways to relax during an attack. They may also take other medicines to control their condition and prevent flare-ups. Extremely severe asthma attacks require immediate medical attention and can lead to death if left untreated.

Outdoor air pollution can bring on asthma attacks. Asthma triggers, or irritants that set off asthma, can include pollution from factories, motor vehicle exhaust, tobacco smoke, and smoke from burning wood or grass. People with asthma are more likely to have severe attacks if they breathe polluted air.

## Reducing Outdoor Air Pollution

People's actions can help everyone breathe better. One way to improve air quality is to use less electricity. When it is hot outside, people can run their air conditioners less and cook with a microwave or toaster oven to help keep their houses cool. During cold weather,

## Breathe: Keeping Your Lungs Healthy

Bike share programs provide a network of bicycles to rent at self-service docking stations in a city. Bicycles are a green alternative to air polluters such as motor vehicles.

people can lower their thermostats and home heating levels. Wearing a sweater or blanket can keep people warm instead. Easy ways to save electricity include using energy-efficient lightbulbs and turning off lights when they are not needed. People can unplug toasters, microwaves, computers, televisions, phone chargers, and other electronics when they are not in use. (Many electrical devices still draw power even when they are turned off.)

Driving less also puts fewer pollutants into the air. Public transportation, such as buses, trains, and subways, can carry a lot more people per trip than a car can. Carpooling to school or work is another good idea. Walking and bicycling are even better because they do not create air pollution. Reducing the use of small-engine motors can improve air quality, too. These outdoor engines usually run on gasoline and are found in lawnmowers, leaf blowers, chain saws, and lawn and garden tractors. Filling a gas tank during the cooler morning or evening hours cuts down on the amount of dangerous gases that move into the air. People should avoid spilling gas and close the gas tank cap tight.

Buying fewer goods means less material ends up as garbage, saving energy. Fossil fuels are needed to make, transport, and get rid of items that people no longer want. Anything wrapped around or attached to a product is packaging that also increases waste. Garbage and even recycling trucks use a lot of gas to pick up waste and truck it to a landfill or recycling center some distance away. If possible,

## Air Quality Awareness for Everyone

The Environmental Protection Agency (EPA) and air quality agencies work together to inform people about air quality in their communities. A key information tool is the Air Quality Index (AQI). Each day the AQI tells how healthy or unhealthy the local air is to breathe and what health effects might occur if someone is outdoors. Every day the EPA determines the AQI based on five major air pollutants: ground-level ozone, particle pollution, carbon monoxide, sulfur dioxide, and nitrogen dioxide. Air pollutants are especially dangerous for children, older adults, and people with asthma or other lung diseases. However, most people find it harder to breathe on unhealthy air days. Even teens playing sports, working in the yard, or cheering for their baseball team can be affected. People can check local air quality levels and air pollution forecasts through local radio, TV, and newspaper weather reports and online at http://airnow.gov.

teens can compost organic materials like food scraps, leaves, and grass clippings at home or a local composting site. Compost can be added to gardens to help plants grow.

Healthy eating habits can reduce air pollution. For example, try to eat food grown locally. It requires less fuel for transporting and is often fresher than food shipped or flown in from another country. People can find locally grown produce at grocery stores, supermarkets, food co-ops, and farmers' markets.

Eating less meat helps improve air quality. More energy from fossil fuels is required to raise 1 pound (.45 kilograms) of meat than one pound of grain. Farmers grow grain to feed animals, and then the animals are processed into meat for people to eat. Finally, the meat is transported to stores. These steps require a lot of energy from fossil fuels, making it more energy-efficient for people to eat grains and vegetables. Saving energy helps reduce air pollution, keeping everyone breathing freely.

# Chapter 4

# Reducing Air Pollutants at Home

Many people enjoy spending time at home. However, the air within some houses and other buildings can be even more polluted than the air outside. For some people, the risk of lung damage may be higher indoors than outdoors. These groups include children, the elderly, and people with respiratory disorders.

The main cause of indoor air pollution is the release of unhealthy gases or particles. One indoor pollutant may not be a problem, but most homes contain a variety of materials that are sources of air pollution. The pollutants can add up in the body over time. By keeping indoor air quality in mind, a family can take many steps to reduce pollution in the home.

## Safe Home Cleaning

Various cleaners are available for keeping a home clean. Many contain synthetic (man-made) chemicals made from fossil fuels. When used, they release an array of pollutants into the air that people inhale. Stores sell a wide variety of cleaners for dishes, sinks, countertops, stoves, ovens, floors, carpets, furniture, windows, and mirrors. Sometimes, silverware, pots, pans, and other

## Breathe: Keeping Your Lungs Healthy

metal objects are polished with special cleaners.

The U.S. Consumer Product Safety Commission (CPSC) oversees the safety of products used in the home. However, the agency has not determined the health risk of most cleaners. In addition, the law does not require companies to list all chemicals on their product labels. People might not realize that many everyday household products used to create clean kitchens, bathrooms, and clothes contain powerful chemicals. Oven cleaners are especially dangerous because they release poisonous fumes. Aerosol sprays change chemicals in oven cleaners into a fine mist. When inhaled, the chemicals can go deep into the lungs and cause damage. Air fresheners and sprays used to cover odors or give a room a certain scent also contain air pollutants.

The "X" on a label indicates that a household product contains potentially harmful chemicals that can inflame the respiratory organs, eyes, or skin at the point of contact.

People should try to avoid breathing fumes from cleaners and polishes, taking care to ventilate a room well when using them (by opening a window or turning on a fan). Families can also reduce their use of synthetic cleaners in the kitchen, bathroom, and other rooms. To stay away from these products, check the labels of cleaners for words like "warning," "caution," "poison," or "danger." The Federal

Hazardous Substances Act (FHSA) requires that household products containing certain dangerous chemicals must say so on the label.

Instead of synthetic cleaners, people can choose cleaning products made with natural minerals, like feldspar and calcite. They can buy castile soap (made from olive oil or other vegetable oils), glycerin soap, or other soaps made from natural ingredients. Families can find cleaning and polishing products that contain plant-based fragrances and dyes and other natural substances, such as sodium silicate or baking soda.

Cleaning products are also in the laundry room. Because they are made from fossil fuels, many laundry detergents and stain removers release unhealthy fumes. Dryer liquids and sheets soften clothing and make it smell good by coating laundry with synthetic fragrances and other chemicals. To reduce the release of chemical fumes, families can find detergents and fabric softeners made from plants, including plant seeds, citrus fruits, vegetable oils, coconut oil, and other natural oils.

A family can easily make their own cleaners for use in the kitchen and other rooms. Common ingredients like baking soda, vinegar, hydrogen peroxide, and plant-based oils work for a variety of cleaning tasks. For example, baking soda or cornstarch mixed with water can remove stains. Books and Web sites about safe and environmentally friendly cleaning can provide information about how to make natural cleaners for the home.

## Lung-Healthy Bedrooms

Many teens spend a lot of time in their bedrooms. There, they sleep, do schoolwork, talk to friends, listen to music, use the Internet, and play games. Making some changes can result in bedrooms that are healthier for the lungs.

Formaldehyde is one of many chemicals released from various synthetic products often found in bedrooms. Other chemicals include acetone, benzene, toluene, and xylene. The risk of health effects from inhaling any of these substances depends on how much is in the air and how long and how often a person breathes the gas. Inhaling even low levels indoors over time may increase the risk of severe asthma attacks or cause breathing problems.

To reduce formaldehyde and other dangerous gas levels in the bedroom, teens can use organic products. Untreated cotton or wool mattresses are available. People can choose bed sheets,

Green Seal is the largest eco-labeling organization in the United States. Products such as these low-odor, zero-VOC paints must meet strict environmental standards to carry the Green Seal label.

# Reducing Air Pollutants at Home

pillowcases, mattress pads, bedspreads, and comforters made from natural materials like cotton, wool, hemp, and bamboo. Some desks, chairs, and furniture that store clothes, books, and other items are made from sustainable (renewable) plants. Some of these plants are abaca (also called bacbac), bamboo, banana leaf, rattan, jute, raffia, rush, sea grass, vetiver root, and hemp. It is important that furniture is made with natural glues, stains, and finishes.

New paint on walls or furniture can change the look of a bedroom quickly. Most paints, though, contain many synthetic chemicals. These chemicals fall into a category of pollutants known as volatile organic compounds (VOCs). The fumes are inhaled as soon as the paint is opened. Newly painted rooms should be aired out until there is no odor. People can also use eco-friendly paints to reduce the health risk to their lungs. Low-VOC and zero-VOC paints emit little or none of these toxic fumes. People can also choose paints made from natural substances, including linseed oil, citrus oils, flour, casein (milk protein), tree resins, waxes, chalk, clay, and quartz.

## Improving Indoor Air Quality

Families can further improve the air quality in their home by following some simple steps. One rule is not to allow any tobacco smoking in the home. Smokers should only smoke outside.

When using household chemicals, people need to follow the label's instructions to reduce air pollution in the home. They can take precautions such as making sure rooms are well ventilated. People should open windows and doors when using synthetic chemicals. Kitchen exhaust fans, which are vented to the outdoors, help reduce the poisons from oven cleaners and other products.

## Dry-Cleaned Clothes

**Dry-cleaned clothes can bring poisonous fumes into the house. To decrease the risk of affecting the lungs, people should remove clothes from dry-cleaning bags and air them outdoors or in a ventilated garage or porch before wearing or storing them. Ask if dry-cleaning shops provide wet cleaning, a safer way to clean clothing. Some items labeled "dry clean only" can be washed with natural products at home. People can also choose clothes that do not require dry cleaning.**

Aerosol products are widely used in the home. However, applying products by spraying increases the chance of inhaling pollutants. The tiny droplets easily enter the blood through the lungs and may harm the lungs and other body tissues. For lung safety, use aerosols in well-ventilated rooms. The best guideline is to avoid sprays in the home whenever possible.

Families should buy only enough household chemicals they can use up in a short period of time. Gases can leak even from closed containers. People need to get rid of old or unneeded cleaners, paints, paint removers, stains, furniture polish, and other chemical products. They can take unused or empty containers to their local solid waste program for disposal.

Personal grooming products like hair spray, hair coloring, shampoos, conditioners, and other hair products are found in many homes. People also use liquid and bar soaps, deodorants, moisturizers, cleansers, and shaving cream. Most of these products are made in factories from fossil fuels and contain synthetic fragrances, colors, detergents, and preservatives. To avoid breathing these chemical fumes, teens can buy personal care products made of organic ingredients like natural herb extracts, minerals, and oils. They can also choose products that are fragrance-free.

## Garages, Lawns, and Gardens

When working in garages, people need to avoid breathing gas and oil fumes. Idling or running cars, trucks, or other equipment in enclosed or attached garages can quickly raise carbon monoxide and other gases to dangerous levels. It is also important to avoid breathing spray paint and paint remover fumes inside a closed garage or workshop. Work in well-ventilated areas. Open doors and windows to bring in fresh air and allow chemical fumes to escape.

Many people enjoy gardening. Some people like a green lawn and growing shrubs, flowers, vegetables, fruits, and herbs. Families may use fertilizers, weed killers, and other chemicals on their lawns or gardens to help plants grow. People may hire lawn services that spray chemicals on the grass to keep it green and thick and apply pesticides to kill bugs. Many of these products release poisonous fumes. Dogs, cats, and children that play on or near treated lawns and gardens may bring the chemicals into the house on their feet. To reduce outdoor pollutants, families can switch to a natural lawn-care service or replace their lawn with an eco-lawn mix of natural grasses, clovers, herbs, and wildflowers. Natural products are available to feed plants and control pests.

Outdoor power equipment such as lawn mowers, hedge trimmers, and leaf blowers produce air pollutants that quickly enter houses through open doors and windows. Whenever possible, families can use manual lawn and garden equipment. Manual mowing, shrub and tree trimming, and leaf raking do not pollute. These activities also provide good exercise!

Breathe: Keeping Your Lungs Healthy

# Ten Great Questions to Ask a Doctor

1. I get frequent colds and respiratory infections. Why does that happen, and how can I prevent them?

2. What vaccinations do I need to keep my lungs healthy?

3. Do I need tests or treatments for allergies?

4. How can I keep my asthma under control?

5. Is it safe to exercise and play sports with asthma? What should I do if I feel short of breath?

6. Would having a dog or cat be OK for me?

7. How can I create a healthy breathing environment in my bedroom?

8. How do healthy lungs look different from a smoker's lungs?

9. How can a person get help quitting smoking?

10. Are there other habits people can change to reduce their risk for lung disease?

# Chapter 5

# A Lifestyle for Healthy Lungs

Lifestyles are key to maintaining and improving the health of the lungs and the respiratory system. Healthy habits, such as increasing physical activity, practicing good hygiene to avoid getting respiratory illnesses, getting flu shots, and reducing stress, keep the lungs performing well. Breathing greatly improves—and the risk of disease declines—when people stop smoking and taking illegal drugs. The goal of lifestyle changes is to develop healthy habits that keep the lungs working properly and help everyone breathe clean air.

## Greater Lung Power with Fitness

Regular physical activity helps the body become and stay strong. The respiratory system works better, resulting in greater levels of oxygen in the blood. The capacity of the lungs increases with exercise. This means teens can climb stairs, ride a bike, or run without feeling out of breath. Exercise also strengthens the heart, causing it to pump oxygen-rich blood to every cell with less effort. In addition, a strong body can more easily fight off germs that cause colds, the flu, and other respiratory illnesses.

    Regular exercise provides other benefits. It can help teens lose weight and maintain a healthy weight, strengthen the muscles and joints, and build strong bones. Teens who get regular exercise generally do better in school because their concentration improves. Many

# Breathe: Keeping Your Lungs Healthy

Lifestyle habits affect the overall health of the lungs. An important habit is doing aerobic exercise, such as running, on a regular basis. The respiratory system works more efficiently with a strong, toned body.

people find that physical activity relieves stress and boosts their mood. They feel more alert and can maintain higher energy levels for longer periods of time.

According to the CDC, teens should get at least sixty minutes of physical activity every day. Most of that time should be spent doing aerobic activity, which strengthens the lungs and heart. Aerobic activity is any physical exercise that uses large muscle groups repeatedly and increases the breathing and heart rates over a period of time. Teens can walk, run, bike, skate, cross-country ski, or dance to get their lungs and heart working faster. They can also get aerobic exercise by playing tennis, shoveling snow from a driveway, mowing the lawn, or taking the dog for a brisk walk. Other aerobic fitness activities include kayaking, canoeing, and swimming laps. Aerobic sports, such as soccer, basketball, hockey, volleyball, and track, are popular among teens.

Muscle strengthening improves muscular fitness and is an important part of an exercise program. Teens need muscle-strengthening activities three or more times a week. Strong muscles take oxygen from the blood more efficiently. This helps the lungs transfer air and waste. Schools and fitness centers offer free weights, weight machines, and other tools for strength training. No special tools are needed when doing crunches, planks, squats, and push-ups at home.

## Caring for the Respiratory System

The respiratory system is a common place of infection. A cold or the flu can sometimes lead to more serious infections like bronchitis and pneumonia. Teens can protect themselves from respiratory infections by washing their hands often with regular soap and water. Using an alcohol-based hand cleaner works, too. People can avoid being near people who are ill, if possible, and avoid sharing their forks and spoons, drinking glasses, and towels. To prevent spreading viruses to others, teens who are sick should stay home from school or work until they feel better. It is a good idea to cough or sneeze into a tissue and then throw it away and wash the hands.

The best way to keep from getting the flu is to get a flu shot every year. Pneumonia, bronchitis, and other complications from the flu can occur even in previously healthy individuals. People with asthma should get vaccinated to decrease the chance of serious complications from the flu. Most people older than six months can get this vaccine, except for those with a severe allergy to eggs or other vaccine components. The new shots are usually available each year beginning in September. A vaccination for pneumonia is also available but is not recommended for everyone. Teens should ask their health care provider which vaccines are recommended for them.

## Posture and Breathing

A simple way to improve breathing is to use good posture. Slouching or leaning forward allows less room for the lungs to function properly. Teens cannot get a good supply of oxygen because they cannot breathe deeply. Balanced posture gives the lungs the best conditions to work efficiently. People can practice good posture by standing, sitting, or walking straight, dropping their shoulders back, and letting their arms and hands hang loosely. Carrying heavy backpacks, purses, or book bags can negatively affect posture and cause neck, shoulder, and back pain.

Even if people are feeling well, having regular checkups can help prevent problems before they start or discover problems early on. This is especially important for lung diseases. Sometimes, they are difficult to detect until they become serious. During a checkup, health care professionals ask many health-related questions and listen to the lungs. Doctors can use a variety of techniques to further examine the lungs to determine if a problem exists and, if so, how to treat it.

## The Lungs and Stress Management

People feel stressed when they are anxious, upset, frustrated, or overwhelmed. Stress is caused by emotions, but it affects every system and organ in the body. Having healthy lungs helps the body respond to stressful situations. When sudden stress occurs, the body prepares itself for a crisis. The lungs take in more oxygen, and the heart pumps more blood containing oxygen to the rest of the body. The brain becomes more alert so that it can respond quickly if a situation is life-threatening. In daily life, though, most events are not extreme emergencies.

Teens can develop and use stress management skills to help them deal with everyday stress. An effective way to handle stress is to do physical activities, such as walking, biking, or playing sports. Some people find stretching, muscle relaxation, meditation, yoga, and tai chi relaxing. Other ways to reduce stress are spending time with friends who are positive, listening to music, journaling, and recalling a happy time, like a day at the beach or a camping trip. Even laughing can decrease tension.

Deep breathing is another way to calm the mind and body. When stressed, people often take short, shallow breaths using the upper chest. Instead, they can practice deep breathing from the diaphragm.

# Breathe: Keeping Your Lungs Healthy

To start, teens can breathe in through the nose and send the air down to the stomach. The lungs fill with air, and the stomach expands a little. Then they can breathe out through the nose, causing the stomach to fall. Deep breathing from the belly every day can strengthen the diaphragm and help people stay relaxed.

Sometimes, people who are stressed choose to get help from others. Reaching out to friends, a family member, or a counselor can be a good start for some teens. Others might want to join a support group for teens to exchange information and learn healthy ways to handle stress.

A teen gives the thumbs-up to green trucks at the Green Long Beach Festival, held annually in Long Beach, California. The event promotes awareness of clean air and other environmental issues in the community.

## Promoting Clean Air

Teens can make changes in their own lives that will help keep the air healthy. They can also become involved in promoting clean air. For example, teens can help other people and organizations make clean air choices by sharing their knowledge about ways to reduce air pollution. They can also join a clean air or environmental organization that focuses on improving air quality. Many of these organizations provide resources to understand current air quality issues.

Writing an article for the school newspaper or writing a letter to a local newspaper or Patch site allows teens to express their opinions about air quality. They can also write to their state representatives and senators, urging them to protect society against air pollution. They can ask their elected officials to support the clean air policies and standards recommended to the EPA by scientists and other experts. All of these changes can add up to everyone having clean air to breathe and healthy lungs.

# GLOSSARY

**addiction** The uncontrollable use of a drug, even though the user knows it is harmful.
**alveolus (plural: alveoli)** A tiny air sac of the lung.
**anesthetic** A substance that causes loss of bodily sensations, typically used to prevent pain during a medical procedure.
**asthma** A lung disease marked by sudden attacks of difficult breathing, wheezing, and coughing. In an asthma attack, the linings of the bronchi swell, narrowing the airways.
**bronchi** The two tubes that connect the larynx to the lungs.
**bronchiole** A tiny tube inside the lungs that ends in alveoli.
**bronchitis** A lung disease that causes coughing and shortness of breath.
**capillary** A tiny blood vessel. Capillaries surround the alveoli in the lungs.
**carbon dioxide** A heavy, colorless gas ($CO_2$) created as a waste product in human and animal respiration and in the decay or burning of organic material. Plants absorb it from the air to create energy during photosynthesis.
**cell** A building block of living things.
**cilia** The microscopic hairlike structures found on the surface of some airways, that wave back and forth.
**circulatory system** The bodily system involved in circulating blood and lymph throughout the body. It includes the heart and blood vessels, such as the arteries, veins, and capillaries.
**cystic fibrosis** An inherited and life-threatening disease that causes respiratory and digestive problems.
**diaphragm** The strong sheet of muscle that separates the chest

cavity from the abdominal cavity in mammals and is the main muscle of respiration.

**emphysema** A disease in which the air sacs of the lungs (alveoli) are grossly enlarged and the tissue is eventually destroyed. Symptoms include shortness of breath, coughing, wheezing, fatigue, and increased risk of infection.

**exhale** To breathe out.

**flu** A contagious viral disease marked by fever, tiredness, severe aches and pains, and inflammation of the respiratory tract.

**inhale** To breathe in.

**larynx** The voice box.

**mucus** A thick, sticky fluid used for moisture and protection in the airways.

**nicotine** An addictive drug contained in tobacco.

**oxygen** An element that is necessary for life, sometimes found as an odorless gas.

**particulate** A substance made up of tiny, separate particles.

**pleural sac** The membrane surrounding the lungs.

**pneumonia** A bacterial infection of the air sacs in the lungs.

**respiratory system** The organs involved in breathing, from nose to lungs.

**secondhand smoke** Tobacco smoke inhaled by nonsmokers who are near smokers.

**tar** A solid residue of tobacco smoke that contains the by-products of burning.

**trachea** The tube in the throat leading to the lungs.

**withdrawal** The process of ridding the body of a drug.

# FOR MORE INFORMATION

American Lung Association
1301 Pennsylvania Avenue NW, Suite 800
Washington, DC 20004
(202) 785-3355
Web site: http://www.americanlungassociation.org
The American Lung Association works to save lives by improving lung health and preventing lung disease.

American Medical Association (AMA)
515 North State Street
Chicago, IL 60654
(800) 621-8335
Web site: http://www.ama-assn.org
The American Medical Association works to promote the art and science of medicine and improve public health.

American Thoracic Society (ATS)
25 Broadway, 18th Floor
New York, NY 10004
(212) 315-8600
Web site: http://www.thoracic.org
This professional and scientific society focuses on respiratory and critical care medicine. The ATS has approximately 12,500 members who help prevent and fight respiratory diseases through research, education, patient care, and advocacy.

## FOR MORE INFORMATION

Centers for Disease Control and Prevention (CDC)
1600 Clifton Road
Atlanta, GA 30333
(800) CDC-INFO [232-4636]
Web site: http://www.cdc.gov
The CDC is a division of the U.S. Department of Health and Human Services. It is an excellent source of information on health, healthy living, and environmental health.

Clean Air Council
135 South 19th Street, Suite 300
Philadelphia, PA 19103
(215) 567-4004
Web site: http://www.cleanair.org
This environmental organization works to protect everyone's right to breathe clean air by ensuring that environmental laws are enforced.

Environmental Defense Fund (EDF)
257 Park Avenue South
New York, NY 10010
(800) 684-3322
Web site: http://www.edf.org
The Environmental Defense Fund focuses on cutting unhealthy air pollution and improving safeguards for toxic chemicals.

**Breathe: Keeping Your Lungs Healthy**

Environmental Working Group (EWG)
1436 U Street NW, Suite 100
Washington, DC 20009
(202) 667-6982
Web site: http://www.ewg.org
This organization works to protect public health and the environment, including keeping the air clean. Its Web site offers useful databases on the safety of household and personal items.

Health Canada
Address Locator 0900C2
Ottawa, ON K1A 0K9
Canada
(866) 225-0709
Web site: http://www.hc-sc.gc.ca
Canada's federal health agency helps people in Canada maintain and improve their health.

Lung Cancer Alliance
888 16th Street NW, Suite 150
Washington, DC 20006
(800) 298-2436
Web site: http://www.lungcanceralliance.org
The Lung Cancer Alliance is the only national nonprofit organization devoted solely to support and advocacy for all those living with or at risk for lung cancer.

## FOR MORE INFORMATION

National Association of Clean Air Agencies (NACAA)
444 North Capitol Street NW, Suite 307
Washington, DC 20001
(202) 624-7864
Web site: http://www.4cleanair.org
This organization represents air pollution control agencies in U.S. states and territories, as well as in 165 major metropolitan areas. It provides current information on important air pollution topics.

National Heart, Lung, and Blood Institute (NHLBI)
NHLBI Health Information Center
P.O. Box 30105
Bethesda, MD 20824-0105
(301) 592-8573
Web site: http://www.nhlbi.nih.gov
The National Heart, Lung, and Blood Institute provides health information related to the lungs, heart, and blood, including information about lung diseases and physical fitness.

National Institutes of Health (NIH)
9000 Rockville Pike
Bethesda, MD 20892
(301) 496-4000
Web site: http://www.nih.gov
The NIH is a division of the U.S. Department of Health and Human Services. It is an excellent source of health information.

Public Health Agency of Canada
130 Colonnade Road
A. L. 6501H
Ottawa, ON K1A 0K9
Canada
(866) 225-0709
Web site: http://www.phac-aspc.gc.ca
The role of the Public Health Agency of Canada is to promote health and prevent and control chronic diseases, including respiratory diseases.

U.S. Environmental Protection Agency (EPA)
Ariel Rios Building
1200 Pennsylvania Avenue NW
Washington, DC 20460
(202) 272-0167
Web site: http://www.epa.gov
The EPA protects human health and the environment and enforces the Clean Air Act.

## Web Sites

Due to the changing nature of Internet links, Rosen Publishing has developed an online list of Web sites related to the subject of this book. This site is updated regularly. Please use this link to access the list:

http://www.rosenlinks.com/hab/brea

# FOR FURTHER READING

Bjornlund, Lydia D. *Teen Smoking* (Compact Research). San Diego, CA: ReferencePoint Press, 2010.

Burstein, John. *The Remarkable Respiratory System: How Do My Lungs Work?* New York, NY: Crabtree Publishing, 2009.

Casper, Julie Kerr. *Fossil Fuels and Pollution: The Future of Air Quality* (Global Warming). New York, NY: Facts on File, 2010.

Caster, Shannon. *Lungs* (Body Works). New York, NY: PowerKids Press, 2010.

Flynn, Noa. *Inhalants and Solvents: Sniffing Disaster* (Illicit and Misused Drugs). Philadelphia, PA: Mason Crest Publishers, 2008.

Gertz, Susan E., Susan Hershberger, and Lynn Hogue. *Breathing Room! Indoor Pollution Activity Handbook* (Strive to Thrive!). Middletown, OH: Terrific Science Press, 2007.

Haerens, Margaret. *Air Pollution* (Global Viewpoints). Detroit, MI: Greenhaven Press/Gale Cengage Learning, 2011.

Higgins, Matt. *The Air Out There: How Clean Is Clean?* (Second Nature). Chicago, IL: Norwood House Press, 2012.

Lew, Kristi. *Respiratory System* (Amazing Human Body). Tarrytown, NY: Marshall Cavendish Benchmark, 2010.

Murphy, Wendy B. *Asthma* (USA Today Health Reports). Minneapolis, MN: Twenty-First Century Books, 2011.

Orr, Tamra. *Respiration: Super Cool Science Experiments* (Science Explorer). Ann Arbor, MI: Cherry Lake Publishing, 2010.

Rapp, Valerie. *Protecting Earth's Air Quality* (Saving Our Living Earth). Minneapolis, MN: Lerner Publications, 2009.

Sheen, Barbara. Lung Cancer (Diseases and Disorders). Detroit, MI: Lucent Books, 2008.

# BIBLIOGRAPHY

Berthold-Bond, Annie. *Home Enlightenment: Practical, Earth-Friendly Advice for Creating a Nurturing, Healthy, and Toxin-Free Home and Lifestyle*. Emmaus, PA: Rodale, 2005.

Centers for Disease Control and Prevention. "Health Effects of Cigarette Smoking." March 21, 2011. Retrieved August 12, 2011 (http://www.cdc.gov/tobacco/data_statistics/fact_sheets/health_effects/effects_cig_smoking).

Centers for Disease Control and Prevention. "Health Effects of Secondhand Smoke." March 21, 2011. Retrieved August 13, 2011 (http://www.cdc.gov/tobacco/data_statistics/fact_sheets/secondhand_smoke/health_effects).

Centers for Disease Control and Prevention. "Inactivated Influenza Vaccine 2011–12: What You Need to Know." July 26, 2011. Retrieved August 20, 2011 (http://www.cdc.gov/vaccines/pubs/vis/downloads/vis-flu.pdf).

Centers for Disease Control and Prevention. "Physical Activity for Everyone: Guidelines: Children." March 30, 2011. Retrieved August 19, 2011 (http://www.cdc.gov/physicalactivity/everyone/guidelines/children.html).

Hollender, Jeffrey, and Alexandra Zissu. *Planet Home: Conscious Choices for Cleaning and Greening the World You Care About Most*. New York, NY: Clarkson Potter Publishers, 2010.

Larsen, Laura. *Environmental Health Sourcebook: Basic Consumer Health Information About the Environment and Its Effects on Human Health* (Health Reference). 3rd ed. Detroit, MI: Omnigraphics, 2010.

Lopez, Ralph I., and Kate Kelly. *The Teen Health Book: A Parents' Guide to Adolescent Health and Well-Being*. New York, NY: W. W. Norton & Co., 2003.

# BIBLIOGRAPHY

Loux, Renée. *Easy Green Living: The Ultimate Guide to Simple, Eco-Friendly Choices for You and Your Home*. Emmaus, PA: Rodale, 2008.

Mayo Clinic. *Mayo Clinic Family Health Book*. Rochester, MN: Time Incorporated, 2009.

National Geographic Society. "Lungs." 2011. Retrieved September 1, 2011 (http://science.nationalgeographic.com/science/health-and-human-body/human-body/lungs-article).

National Institute on Drug Abuse. "Cocaine—InfoFacts." March 2010. Retrieved August 14, 2011 (http://drugabuse.gov/infofacts/cocaine.html).

National Institute on Drug Abuse. "Marijuana—InfoFacts." November 2010. Retrieved August 13, 2011 (http://drugabuse.gov/infofacts/marijuana.html).

Newton, David E. *Chemistry of the Environment* (The New Chemistry). New York, NY: Facts on File, 2007.

Parker, Steve. *The Human Body Book*. New York, NY: DK Publishing, 2007.

Ross, Benjamin, and Steven Amter. *The Polluters: The Making of Our Chemically Altered Environment*. New York, NY: Oxford University Press, 2010.

Schoff, Jill Potvin. *Green-Up Your Cleanup* (Green House). Upper Saddle River, NJ: Creative Homeowner, 2008.

Steen, Bill. "Make Safe, Natural Paint." *Mother Earth News*, October/November 2006. Retrieved August 13, 2011 (http://www.motherearthnews.com/Do-It-Yourself/2006-10-01/Make-Safe-Natural-Paint.aspx).

U.S. Consumer Product Safety Commission and U.S. Environmental Protection Agency. "The Inside Story: A Guide to Indoor Air Quality." 2011. Retrieved August 15, 2011 (http://www.cpsc.gov/cpscpub/pubs/450.html).

U.S. Environmental Protection Agency. "About Air Toxics—Toxic Air Pollutants—Air and Radiation." August 11, 2011. Retrieved August 18, 2011 (http://www.epa.gov/air/toxicair/newtoxics.html).

U.S. Environmental Protection Agency. "Air Quality Index (AQI): A Guide to Air Quality and Your Health." September 3, 2010. Retrieved August 10, 2011 (http://www.airnow.gov/index.cfm?action=aqibasics.aqi).

U.S. Environmental Protection Agency. "The Inside Story: A Guide to Indoor Air Quality." April 18, 2011. Retrieved August 12, 2011 (http://www.epa.gov/iaq/pubs/insidestory.html).

U.S. Environmental Protection Agency. "The Plain English Guide to the Clean Air Act—Air and Radiation." April 29, 2008. Retrieved August 17, 2011 (http://www.epa.gov/air/peg/index.html).

# INDEX

## A

acetone, 38
addiction, 15, 17, 22–24
  treatment programs for, 24
aerobic activity, 45
aerosol products, 21, 36, 39–40
air pollution, 13, 26
  asthma and, 13, 31, 33, 38
  common air pollutants, 26–31
  reducing indoor pollutants, 35–41
  reducing outdoor pollutants, 31–34, 41
Air Quality Index (AQI), 33
alveoli, 9, 10–11, 16, 29
asthma, 13, 18, 31, 33, 38, 46

## B

bedrooms, reducing pollutants in, 37–39
benzene, 38
bronchi (bronchial tubes), 9, 11, 12, 16, 29
bronchioles, 9, 29

## C

capillaries, 9, 10
carbon dioxide, 9, 10–11, 28
carbon monoxide, 16, 28–29, 33, 41
chronic bronchitis/bronchitis, 16, 19, 29, 30, 45, 46
chronic obstructive lung disease (COPD), 16
cigarette smoking, 13, 14–17, 18, 22, 24, 28, 31, 39, 43
cilia, 12, 15, 16, 29–30
circulatory system, 6, 9, 15, 18, 24
cleaning products, 19, 35–37, 40
cocaine, 14, 18–19, 22
crack, 19, 22
cystic fibrosis, 16

## D

diaphragm, 8–9, 48
drugs and the lungs, 14, 18–24, 43
dry cleaning/dry-cleaned clothes, 40

## E

emphysema, 13, 16, 30
Environmental Protection Agency (EPA), 33, 49
epiglottis, 9
esophagus, 9
exercise, 43–45, 47

## F

Federal Hazardous Substances Act (FHSA), 36–37
flu/flu shots, 43, 45, 46
formaldehyde, 38
fossil fuels, burning of, 27, 28, 29

## G

gardening products, 41
gas and oil fumes, 41
gases, pollution and, 27–29, 35
gas exchange process, 9–11
glottis, 12

## H

heart, 6, 8, 9, 10, 17, 19, 21, 22, 43, 45, 47

## I

inhalants, 14, 19–22

## L

larynx (voice box), 12
lung cancer, 13, 16–17, 18
lung capacity, 6–8, 43
lungs
  air pollution and, 13, 26, 28–31, 33, 35–41
  anatomy of, 6–8
  cigarette smoking and, 13, 14–16, 17–18, 22, 24, 28, 31, 43
  diseases of, 16–18
  drugs and, 14, 18–24, 43
  exercise and, 43–45
  functions of, 4, 6, 9, 11–12
  how they work, 8–9
speech and, 12
  stress and, 43, 47–49
lung transplants, 24–25

## M

macrophages, 12
marijuana, 14, 18–19, 22
metals, pollution and, 30–31
mucus, 12, 15, 16, 18, 19, 29, 31
muscle-strengthening activities, 45

## N

nicotine, 14, 15, 17, 22
nitrogen oxides, 28, 29, 33

## O

outdoor power equipment, 33, 41
oxygen, 4, 6, 9–10, 13, 16, 21, 27, 28, 29, 43, 45, 46, 47
ozone, 27, 29, 33

## P

paints, 39, 40, 41
particulate matter, pollution and, 27, 29–31, 33, 35
personal grooming products, 40
pharynx (throat), 9
physical addiction, 22
pleural sac, 8
pneumonia, 13, 29, 45, 46
posture, 46
psychological addiction, 22
pulmonary arteries, 10
pulmonary veins, 9–10

## R

relaxation techniques, 47
reserve air, 25
residual air, 25
respiratory infections, protection from, 45–46
respiratory system, 4, 6, 9, 11, 14, 15, 18, 19, 21, 24, 28, 29, 43, 45–47
rib bones, 8

## S

secondhand smoke, 18
smog, 26–27, 29
stress
  lungs and, 43, 47–49
  management/reduction of, 45, 47–48
sudden sniffing death, 21
sulfur dioxide, 28, 29, 33

## INDEX

### T
tar, 15–16
teeth brushing, 13
temperature regulation of air, 11
toluene, 38
trachea (windpipe), 9, 11, 12, 29
treatment programs for addiction,
 types of, 24

### V
vocal cords, 12
volatile organic compounds (VOCs), 39

### W
withdrawal, 22

### X
xylene, 38

## About the Author

Judy Monroe Peterson has earned two master's degrees, including one in public health education, and is the author of more than sixty educational books for young people. She is a former health care, technical, and academic librarian and college faculty member; a biologist and research scientist; and curriculum writer and editor with more than twenty-five years of experience. She has taught courses at 3M, the University of Minnesota, and Lake Superior College. Currently, she is a writer and editor of K–12 and post–high school curriculum materials on a variety of subjects, including health, life skills, biology, life science, and the environment.

## Photo Credits

Cover © www.istockphoto.com/shadrin_audrey; p. 5 M. Nader/The Image Bank/Getty Images; p. 7 Anita Potter/Shutterstock.com; p. 10 3D Clinic/Getty Images; p. 11 SPL/Photo Researchers; p. 15 Robert Kneschke/Shutterstock.com; p. 17 AFP Graphics Service/Newscom; p. 20 Biophoto Associates/Photo Researchers; p. 23 © AP Images; p. 27 Justin Lambert/The Image Bank/Getty Images; p. 28 © www.istockphoto.com/milehightraveler; p. 30 Alila Sao Mai/Shutterstock.com; p. 32 Chang W. Lee/The NewYork Times/Redux; p. 36 Digital Vision/Thinkstock; p. 38 © Ambient Images, Inc./SuperStock; p. 44 A. Turner/Shutterstock.com; p. 48 Frank Siteman/Science Faction/Getty Images; p. 48 © Kayle Deioma/PhotoEdit; cover (background graphic), interior graphic (frame) © www.istockphoto.com/liquidplanet; interior graphic (human organs) © www.istockphoto.com/bubaone; interior graphic (ECG waves) © www.istockphoto.com/linearcurves.

Designer: Nicole Russo; Editor: Andrea Sclarow Paskoff;
Photo Researcher: Marty Levick